About the

Canadian born Suzan St Maur has lived [...] early career start in journalism on a lo[...] allegiances to advertising and later becam[...] business television and live events. Today [...] media for a wide variety of business co[...]nication purposes, as well as training and lecturing on how to write more powerfully for business. In addition she has written several published non-fiction books on consumer and business topics. Her first joke book, *The Horse Lover's Joke Book*, was also published by Kenilworth Press, in 2001.

When growing up in Canada, Suzan shared her early life with anything up to twenty-four dogs at one time, as her parents bred Boxers and American Cocker Spaniels. Today Suzan lives in the Bedfordshire countryside with her young son plus a horse, two cats, a few goldfish in the pond, and just two dogs – both 'rescues' of indeterminate pedigree, and probably the two most-loved dogs in the whole of England.

Canine Capers

Over 350 jokes to make your tail wag

Suzan St Maur

KENILWORTH PRESS

To my Mother
... who brought me up together with
Boxer and Spaniel puppies and only told me I
was human when I learned to say something
other than 'woof ...'

First published in Great Britain 2002 by
Kenilworth Press
Addington
Buckingham
MK18 2JR

British Library Cataloguing in Publication Data
A CIP record for this book is available from the British Library

ISBN 1-872119-50-6

Illustrations by Pam Tanzey

Typesetting and layout by Kenilworth Press
Printed and bound in Great Britain by Bell & Bain Ltd, Glasgow

Preface

Hello and welcome to my second joke book – my first collection of doggy jokes.

Reams and reams (or should it be gigabytes and gigabytes?) have been written about 'man's best friend', and quite rightly so. In my view dogs often make far better, more loyal and even more intelligent friends than some of the humans you come across.

Many of us have had lots of dogs in our lifetimes but (if you're like me) there are a select few whom you remember as being extra special. In my case, they were Wolfie, Hum-Hum, and Boswell – a GSD, English Setter and Labrador respectively. Wherever you are, boys, I hope you're enjoying the most wonderful walkies in the sky.

And let this little book be a tribute to all the canine creatures who have, do and will give our lives the extra dimension that no human could ever hope to parallel.

(We may laugh, but we're laughing about ourselves, not you. Yes, we are. And here's a 'bicky' to prove it ...)

SUZAN ST MAUR

★ Snowstorm

A Great Dane and a Miniature Dachshund were out walking one winter day, and got caught in an unexpected snowstorm. As they hurried for home, the Great Dane complained, 'Goodness me, my feet are cold.'

The Dachshund shivered, looked up at his friend and replied crossly, 'So you think you have a problem ...'

★ Limp

Two men were approaching each other in the street, and each noticed that the other was limping badly. As they drew level with one another, the first man said, 'What happened to you?'

'Falkland Islands, 1982. You?'

'Dog poo, ten minutes ago.'

★ Poker face

A foreign tourist visiting London entered a pub in the East End and, on his way to find the toilets, accidentally walked into a room where several people were gathered together playing poker. This was obviously a serious game as there were large piles of money on the table. The tourist was amazed to see that one of the players was a German Shepherd.

'That's incredible,' said the tourist. 'Can this dog really play poker?'

'Yes,' replied one of the human players. 'But he's not much good. We always know when he's got a good hand because he wags his tail.'

★ Dead weight

A man took his Great Dane to see the vet. 'My dog's got a watering eye. Is there anything you can do for him?'

'Well,' said the vet, 'let's have a look.' She picked the dog up and examined his eyes, then checked his teeth. Finally, she said, 'I'm going to have to put him down.'

'Why? Because he has a watering eye?'

'No, because he's incredibly heavy.'

★ Quick thinking

A wealthy man decided to go on a safari in Africa. He took his faithful Cocker Spaniel along for company. One day the dog started to chase butterflies and before long he discovered that he was lost. So, wandering about, he noticed a leopard heading rapidly in his direction with the obvious intention of having lunch.

The dog thought, 'Gosh, I'm in deep poo now.' Then he noticed some bones on the ground close by, and immediately settled down to chew on the bones with his back to the approaching cat.

Just as the leopard was about to leap, the dog exclaimed loudly, 'My, that was one delicious leopard. I wonder if there are any more around here?'

Hearing this the leopard halted his attack in mid stride, as a look of terror came over him, and slunk away into the trees.

'Whew', said the leopard. 'That was close. That dog nearly had me.'

Meanwhile, a monkey who had been watching the whole scene from a nearby tree, reckoned he could put this knowledge to good use and swap it for protection from the leopard. So, off he went. But the dog saw him running after the leopard at high speed, and realised that something must be up.

The monkey soon caught up with the leopard, spilt the beans and struck a deal for himself with the leopard. The leopard was furious at being made a fool of and said, 'Here monkey, hop on my back and see what's going to happen to that conniving canine.'

Now the dog saw the leopard coming with the monkey on his

9

back, and thought, 'What am I going to do now?' But instead of running, the dog sat down with his back to his attackers pretending he hadn't seen them yet. And just when they got close enough to hear, the dog said, 'Where's that monkey. I just can never trust him. I sent him off half an hour ago to bring me another leopard, and he's still not back!'

★ Hotels

A woman wrote to a hotel on the Isle of Wight prior to booking her holiday there, asking if they would allow her to bring her Cairn terrier.

A few days later she received a letter from the hotel which said:

Dear Madam,

This hotel has been established since 1902. Not once in its history have its proprietors been obliged to ring the police to eject a disorderly dog from the bar, to request repeatedly that a dog should turn down the noise from the television, to deal with a dog's endless complaints about the quality of food and service, or to suffer a bounced cheque written by a dog. Similarly, no dog has ever been found to have set the bedclothes on fire from having fallen asleep with a lit cigarette, nor has a dog ever been responsible for stealing towels, bathrobes, ashtrays, the Gideon's Bible or the telephone directory from a room. We conclude, therefore, by informing you that your dog will be most welcome at our hotel. And if the dog can vouch for its owner, you, too, will be most welcome.

★ Day out

A breeder was taking a car load of West Highland White Terriers to a dog show. Just a few miles from the show venue her car broke down, so she hailed a passing taxi which fortunately was empty, and said to the driver she'd give him £100 if he'd take the dogs to the show. The cab driver loaded the dogs up and went off, and the breeder started the long wait for the breakdown service to turn up.

About an hour later she was amazed to see the taxi come back and stop beside her, the Westies bouncing excitedly and yapping in the back seat. She shouted out 'But I gave you £100 to take them to the show!' The cab driver shouted back 'Oh, but the tickets only came to £50. So I'll take them ten-pin bowling now.'

★ Meat

A butcher was working, and was really busy. He noticed a black Labrador in his shop and shooed him away. Later, he realised that the dog was back again. He walked over to the dog, and saw that the dog had a note in his mouth. The butcher took the note, and it read, 'Can I have twelve sausages and a leg of lamb, please.'

The butcher looked, and lo and behold, in the dog's mouth there was a ten pound note. So the butcher took the money, put the sausages and lamb in a bag, and placed it in the dog's mouth. The butcher was very impressed, and since it was closing time, he decided to shut up shop and follow the dog.

The dog was walking down the road and came to a crossing. The dog put down the bag, jumped up and pressed the crossing button. Then he waited patiently, bag in mouth, for the lights to change. They did, and he walked across the road, with the butcher following.

The dog then came to a bus stop, and started looking at the timetable. The butcher was in awe at this stage. The dog checked out the times, and sat on one of the seats to wait for the bus.

Along came a bus. The dog looked at the number, noticed it was the right bus, and climbed on. The butcher, by now open-mouthed, followed him on to the bus.

The bus travelled through the town and out to the suburbs. Eventually the dog got up, moved to the front of the bus and, standing on his hind legs, pushed the button to stop the bus. The dog got off, shopping still in his mouth, and the butcher still following.

They walked down the road, and the dog approached a house. He walked up the footpath, and dropped the shopping on the step. Then he walked back down the path, took a big run, and threw himself – whap!- against the door. He went back down the path, took another run, and threw himself – whap! – against the door again.

There was no reply at the door, so the dog went back down the path, jumped up on a narrow wall, and walked along the perimeter of the garden. He got to a window, and banged his head against it several times. He walked back, jumped off the wall, and waited at the door.

The butcher watched as a huge man opened the door, and started shouting at the dog.

The butcher ran up and stopped the guy. 'What on earth are you doing? This dog is a genius. He could be on television, for God's sake!'

To which the man responded, 'Clever, my foot. This is the second time this week he's forgotten his keys!'

★ Famous dog quotes

'If your dog is fat, you aren't getting enough exercise' – *Unknown*

'Some days you're the dog; some days you're the lamp post.' – *Unknown*

'Whoever said you can't buy happiness forgot about puppies.' – *Gene Hill*

'In dog years, I'm dead.' – *Unknown*

'To his dog, every man is Napoleon; hence the constant popularity of dogs.' – *Aldous Huxley*

'A dog teaches a boy fidelity, perseverance, and to turn around three times before lying down.' – *Robert Benchley*

'I loathe people who keep dogs. They are cowards who haven't got the guts to bite people themselves.' – *August Strindberg*

'No animal should ever jump up on the dining room furniture unless absolutely certain that he can hold his own in the conversation.' – *Fran Lebowitz*

'Ever consider what they must think of us? I mean, here we come back from a grocery store with the most amazing haul – chicken, pork, half a cow. They must think we're the greatest hunters on earth!' – *Anne Tyler*

'I wonder if other dogs think poodles are members of a weird religious cult.' – *Rita Rudner*

'My dog is worried about the economy because Alpo is up to 99 cents a can. That's almost $7.00 in dog money.' – *Joe Weinstein*

'If I have any beliefs about immortality, it is that certain dogs I have known will go to heaven, and very, very few persons.' – *James Thurber*

'You enter into a certain amount of madness when you marry a person with pets.' – *Nora Ephron*

'Don't accept your dog's admiration as conclusive evidence that you are wonderful.' – *Ann Landers*

'Did you ever walk into a room and forget why you walked in? I think that's how dogs spend their lives.' – *Sue Murphy*

Why did I come in here?

'Women and cats will do as they please, and men and dogs should relax and get used to the idea.' – *Robert A. Heinlein*

'In order to keep a true perspective of one's importance, everyone should have a dog that will worship him and a cat that will ignore him.' – *Dereke Bruce, Taipei, Taiwan*

'Of all the things I miss from veterinary practice, puppy breath is one of the most fond memories!' – *Dr Tom Cat*

'There is no psychiatrist in the world like a puppy licking your face.' – *Ben Williams*

'When a man's best friend is his dog, that dog has a problem.' – *Edward Abbey*

'Cat's motto: No matter what you've done wrong, always try to make it look like the dog did it.' – *Unknown*

'Money will buy you a pretty good dog, but it won't buy the wag of his tail.' – *Unknown*

'No one appreciates the very special genius of your conversation as the dog does.' – *Christopher Morley*

'A dog is the only thing on earth that loves you more than he loves himself.' – *Josh Billings*

'Man is a dog's idea of what God should be.' – *Holbrook Jackson*

'The average dog is a nicer person than the average person.' – *Andrew A. Rooney*

'He is your friend, your partner, your defender, your dog. You are his life, his love, his leader. He will be yours, faithful and true, to the last beat of his heart. You owe it to him to be worthy of such devotion.' – *Unknown*

'If you pick up a starving dog and make him prosperous, he will not bite you; that is the principal difference between a dog and a man.' – *Mark Twain*

'Things that upset a terrier may pass virtually unnoticed by a Great Dane.' – *Smiley Blanton*

'I've seen a look in dogs' eyes, a quickly vanishing look of amazed contempt, and I am convinced that basically dogs think humans are nuts.' – *John Steinbeck*

★ God and dog

On the first day of creation, God created dog.

On the second day of creation, God created man to serve the dog.

On the third day of creation, God created all other animals of the earth to serve as potential food for the dog.

On the fourth day of creation, God created honest toil so man could labour for the good of the dog.

On the fifth day of creation, God created the rubber ball so that the dog might or might not fetch it.

On the sixth day of creation, God created veterinary medicine to keep the dog healthy and the man insolvent.

On the seventh day of creation God tried to rest. But He had to take the dog for a walk.

★ Dog's little friends

An over-zealous advertising executive had been told to conduct extensive research into fleas and how they might be trained to use in an innovative advertising campaign for a prospective client.

He carefully captured a large flea from his dog's back, and – working late into the night over several days – trained the flea to jump over his finger every time he yelled, 'Up!' Once he had accomplished this he pulled two of the flea's six legs off. 'Up!' he yelled. The flea jumped over his finger once again. Off came two more flea legs. 'Up!' he shouted. Again the flea jumped. Finally, he pulled off the flea's remaining two legs. Unfortunately, this time when he yelled 'Up!' the flea didn't move.

Deeply concerned, the advertising executive concluded that fleas would be hard to train for use in any advertising campaign because, as he wrote in his feedback report, 'When a flea loses all six of its legs, it becomes deaf.'

★ Sniffer dog

A man was seated in a plane which was about to take off, when another man with a large German Shepherd took up the empty seats beside him.

The dog was sitting in the middle. The first man looked enquiringly at the dog, so the second man explained to him that they both worked for the airline.

The dog handler said 'Don't mind Bonzo. He's a sniffer dog – the best in the business. You'll see what I mean when we're airborne and I set him to work.'

The plane took off and levelled out. Now, the handler said to the first man, 'Watch this.' He said to the dog 'Bonzo, search.'

The dog jumped down, walked along the aisle and sat next to a woman for a few seconds. It then returned to its seat and put one paw on the handler's arm. 'Good boy,' said the handler.

He turned to the first man and said, 'That woman is in possession of marijuana, so I'm making a note of this for the police who will arrest her when we land.'

'Incredible!' replied the first man.

Once again the handler sent the dog to search the aisles. The dog

19

sniffed around, sat down beside a man for a few seconds, returned to its seat and placed both paws on the handler's arm.

The handler said, 'That man is carrying cocaine, so again, I'm making a note of this.'

'Amazing!' said the first man.

Yet again the handler sent the dog to search the aisles. Bonzo trotted up and down the aisle of the aircraft and after a while sat down next to someone, then came racing back, jumped up onto his seat and urinated profusely.

The first man was surprised and disgusted by this, so he asked the handler, 'What's the problem?'

'Well,' the handler replied nervously, 'I expect he's just found a bomb!'

★ Lapping it up

In front of a dingy petshop, an art connoisseur noticed a mangy little mongrel puppy lapping up milk from a bowl. The bowl, he realised with a start, was a very rare and precious piece of porcelain.

He walked into the petshop and offered ten pounds for the puppy. 'It's not for sale,' said the proprietor.

'Look,' said the collector, 'that puppy is dirty and probably ill with distemper or worse, but I'm eccentric. I like puppies that way. I'll raise my offer to twenty pounds.'

'Done,' said the proprietor, and pocketed the twenty pounds on the spot.

'For that sum I'm sure you won't mind throwing in the bowl,' said the connoisseur. 'The puppy seems so happy drinking from it.'

'No way,' said the proprietor firmly. 'That's my lucky bowl. From that bowl, so far this week I've sold twelve puppies.'

★ Equal opportunities

A small business in a provincial town needed some help with office admin. The manager put a sign in the front window, saying: 'HELP REQUIRED. Must be good at word processing and spreadsheet work, and must be bilingual. We are an Equal Opportunities Employer.'

Soon afterwards, a Bearded Collie trotted up to the window, saw the sign and went inside. He looked at the receptionist and wagged his tail, then walked over to the sign, looked at it and whined.

Guessing what the dog meant, the receptionist called the manager. The manager looked at the dog and was surprised, to say the least.

However, the dog looked determined, so the manager showed him into the office. Inside, the dog jumped up on the chair and stared at the manager.

The manager said, 'I can't employ you. The job spec says you must be good at word processing.' The dog jumped down, went to the keyboard and proceeded to key in and print out a perfect letter. He carefully took the page out of the printer in his teeth, trotted over to the manager and gave it to him, then jumped back up on the chair. The manager was amazed, but then told the dog, 'The job spec says you have to be good with spreadsheet work.'

The dog jumped down again and went back to the computer. The dog proceeded to enter and execute a perfect spreadsheet calculation that balanced perfectly. By this time the manager was totally dumbfounded.

He looked at the dog and said, 'I can see that you are a very intelligent dog and have some interesting abilities. However, I still can't give you the job.' The dog jumped down and went over to a copy of the job spec, putting his put his paw on the sentence about their being an Equal Opportunities Employer. The manager said, 'Yes, but the job spec also says that you must be bilingual'.

The dog wagged his tail, looked up at the manager and said, 'Meow.'

★ Clever stuff

Four men were boasting about how clever their dogs were. One was an engineer, the second man was an accountant, the third was a pharmacist, and the fourth was a government worker.

To show off, the engineer called to his dog, 'T-Square, do your trick!' T-Square trotted over to a desk, took out some paper and a pen and promptly drew a square, circle and triangle.

Everyone agreed that was clever. But the accountant said his dog could do better.

He called to his dog and said, 'Spreadsheet, do your trick.' Spreadsheet went into the kitchen and returned with a dozen chocolate biscuits. He then divided them into four equal piles of three biscuits each.

Everyone agreed that was good. Then the pharmacist said his dog could do better. He called to his dog and said, 'Measure, do your trick.'

Measure got up, walked over to the fridge, took out a litre of milk, got a 400 millilitre glass from the sideboard and poured exactly 300 millilitres without spilling a drop.

Everyone agreed that was very impressive. The three men turned to the government worker and said, 'What can your dog do?' The government worker called to his dog and said, 'Tea Break, do your trick.'

Tea Break jumped to his feet, ate the chocolate biscuits, drank the milk, urinated on the paper, mounted the other three dogs, stated that he injured his back while doing so, formally notified his Trades Union that he was the victim of an industrial accident, applied for Legal Aid to help him claim more than a million pounds in compensation, and then went home for the rest of the day on sick leave.

'That's not merely clever,' they all said in unison. 'That dog is brilliant.'

★ East-West divide

At the height of the arms race, the Americans and Russians realised that, if they continued, before long they would finish up by destroying the world. So they discussed the issue at a top secret summit meeting and decided to settle the whole argument with a dogfight.

The negotiators agreed that each country would take five years to develop the best fighting dog they could. The winning dog would earn its country the right to rule the world. The losing country would have to lay down its arms.

The Russians found the biggest, fiercest Dobermans and Rottweilers in all of the Soviet Union. They cross-bred them and then crossed their offspring with the fiercest Siberian wolves. They selected only the biggest, strongest puppy from the final litter, removed all the other puppies and left the lone dog to grow strong and large. They used steroids and rigorous training in aggression and ruthless killing power. Finally when the five years were up, they had a dog that oozed murder from every pore and had to be restrained in cage made from steel girders. Only the trainers could handle this beast, and even they had to exercise extreme caution.

When the day of the final fight dawned, the Americans arrived with a bizarre animal. It was a nine-foot-long Basset Hound. The Russians pitied the Americans. None of them thought this weird dog stood a chance against the growling monster in the Russian cage. Bookies around the world lay very short odds on the Russians winning in a matter of seconds.

The cages were opened and the dogs released. The Basset Hound waddled towards the middle of the ring. The Russian dog leapt from his cage and charged the giant sausage-dog.

The moment the two dogs met, the Basset Hound opened its jaws and consumed the Russian monster in one mouthful. There was nothing left but a few tufts of fur from the Russian dog's tail.

The Russians walked over to the Americans, blinking their eyes in disbelief. 'We cannot comprehend. Our foremost scientists and trainers laboured for five years with the strongest, fiercest

Dobermans, Rottweilers and Siberian wolves. They created a killing machine.'

'You don't say,' the Americans replied. 'Well, we got our foremost cosmetic surgeons labouring for five years to make a crocodile look like a Basset Hound.'

★ Licence

Some years ago the British Government decided to crack down on dog owners who had not purchased licences for their pets. Police were given instructions to stop dog owners at random and check the licences or warn them to go and buy one.

One elderly gentleman who was stopped asked the policeman what the problem was. The officer pointed to a large Old English Sheepdog sitting in the passenger seat and said, 'Does your dog have a licence?''Oh, no,' replied the elderly man. 'He doesn't need one, because I always drive.'

★ Manage that

Once upon a time there was a shepherd looking after his sheep by a quiet country road. Suddenly a brand new Mitsubishi Shogun screeched to a halt next to him. The driver, a young man dressed in a designer suit, Gucci shoes, Ray-Ban glasses and a YSL tie, got out and asked the shepherd, 'If I guess how many sheep you have, will you give one of them to me?'

The shepherd looked at the young man, then looked at the sheep which were grazing beyond and said, 'All right'.

The young man parked the car, connected to the internet on his PDA, entered a NASA site, scanned the ground using his direct GPS link, opened a data base and 60 Excel tables filled with algorithms, then printed out a 24-slide PowerPoint presentation summarising his conclusions using his high-tech mini-printer. He then turned to the shepherd and said, 'You have exactly eight hundred and seventy-three sheep here.'

The shepherd answered, 'That's correct, you can have your sheep.'

The young man took the animal and put it in the back of his Shogun.

The shepherd looked at the young man and asked, 'If I guess your profession, will you return my sheep to me?'

The young man answered, 'Yes, why not?'

The shepherd said, 'You are a management consultant'.

'How did you know?' asked the young man.

'Very simple,' answered the shepherd. 'First you come here without being called. Second, you charge me a sheep to tell me something I already know. Third, you do not understand anything about what I do, because you took my Border Collie.'

★ Papers

Over breakfast one morning, a husband and wife were discussing their Kerry Blue Terrier. 'Barney is so clever,' she said. 'Every morning when we let him out he brings the newspapers in for us.'

Her husband chewed on a piece of toast. 'Mind you, virtually any dog can do that.'

'Ah,' replied his wife, 'but we've never ordered or subscribed to any.'

★ Trick question

Two psychometric testing experts were discussing the merits and demerits of the various questions they included in the tests they issued to candidates.

'There are some questions that obtain strange responses,' said one. 'I'll give you an example. What would you reply to this: what do men do standing up, that women do sitting down, and dogs do on three legs?'

'Well, shake hands, of course,' replied the other expert.

'Absolutely right,' said the first expert. 'But you'd be shocked by some of the responses I get to that one.'

★ Dog Appreciation Week

To celebrate this year's Dog Appreciation Week, here's a list of ten special treats you can do for your dog ... things he (or she) will truly appreciate:

1. Lick his face and whine appreciatively.

2. If you have a Labrador, bring him the smelliest wellington boot from your utility room.

3. Get him a juicy bone from the butcher's and bury it for him.

4. Make a concerted effort to learn how to howl.

5. Eat your supper on the floor with him (and remember, no hands).

6. Spend quality time with him by rolling with him in adjacent patches of fox poo.

7. Beat him to the door when the postman arrives and growl with him.

8. Get some new plants for your garden and let him dig the holes.

9. Let him sleep on your bed (and remember to share the duvet).

10. Banish your cat to the garden shed for the entire week.

★ Lying

A clergyman was walking down the street when he ran into a group of a few boys, all about ten years old. They were clustered around a small mongrel dog. Worried that the boys might be hurting the dog, the clergyman went over and asked them what they were doing.

'This dog is an old neighbourhood stray,' said one of the boys. 'We take him home with us sometimes, but only one of us can take him home. So we're having a competition. Whichever one of us tells the biggest lie can take him home today.'

Naturally the clergyman was shocked. 'You boys shouldn't be having a lie-telling competition,' he admonished. He then launched into a ten-minute sermon about the evils of lying. 'Don't you boys know it's a sin to lie?' he started off and ten minutes later ended with, 'You know, when I was your age, I never told a lie.'

There was complete silence for about a minute. As the clergyman smiled with satisfaction at the thought of having got through to them, the youngest boy gave a deep sigh. 'All right,' he said, looking around at his friends, 'give him the dog.'

★ Washing up

The local Vicar was invited to tea with a family in his parish, and he reluctantly agreed to go, despite knowing that their standards of hygiene left something to be desired. As he sat down at the table he noticed that the plates and other crockery were very grubby indeed.

'Do you wash up your crockery, Mrs Johnson?' asked the Vicar as kindly as he could manage.

'Of course I do, Vicar,' smiled Mrs Johnson. 'They're as clean as soap and water could make them.'

The Vicar said Grace and ate his tea, enjoying it thoroughly as it was delicious irrespective of the dirty plates. However his enjoyment was rather spoiled when, after tea was finished, Mrs Johnson piled up the plates and took them out to the kitchen shouting, 'Come on, dogs! Here, Soap! Here, Water!'

★ Good marriage

A man brought his new boss home for dinner one evening. As they arrived at the door the man's wife ran up, flung her arms around her husband and kissed him passionately.

'Goodness me,' said his boss, 'and how long have you been married?'

'Twenty-four years,' replied the man.

'You must have a wonderful marriage for your wife to greet you like that after all those years.'

'Not really. She only does it to make the dog jealous.'

★ Quickies

Advertisement in local newspaper: 'GSD puppies for sale to good homes only. Will eat anything, love children.'

'My dog can play chess, you know.'
  'No kidding? He must be very clever.'
  'Not really. I nearly always win.'

Teacher: 'Does anyone know what "dogma" means?'
Pupil: 'Yes miss, it's a female dog who's just had puppies.'

Sign on the door of a veterinary practice: 'BACK IN TEN MINUTES. SIT! STAY!'

Mum: 'Take that dog out of the house, it's full of fleas.
Little boy: 'Come on out of the house, Max, it's full of fleas.'

Woman 1: 'Our spaniel is just like one of the family.'
Woman 2: 'Really? Which one?'

My dog can read signs, you know. In fact the other day in the High Street he saw a sign saying 'wet paint'. So he did.

Teacher: 'Can someone tell me what a comet is?'
Pupil: 'A star with a tail.'
Teacher: 'Well done. Now can you name one?'
Pupil: 'Lassie.'

★ Business prediction

Many manufacturing businesses in the future, though very large, will only require two employees to maintain their everyday function – just one human, and one dog. The human will be there to feed the dog, and the dog will be there to prevent the human from touching the computers.

★ Riddles

What breed of dog did Count Dracula prefer?
Bloodhounds.

Why does a dog scratch himself?
Because he can't tell anyone else where it itches.

Where should you never take a dog?
To a flea market.

What do you call a dog who can tell the time?
A watch dog.

Which breed of dog likes being bathed the most?
Shampoodle.

What do get if you cross a dog with an insolvency practitioner?
A Golden Receiver.

Which button on a DVD player is the easiest for a dog to use?
The paws button.

Why did the Dalmatian go to the dry cleaner's?
Because his coat was covered in spots.

Why does a dog turn round several times before settling down?
Because one good turn deserves another.

What's the best way to stop a dog smelling?
Hold its nose.

Why did the woman take her dog to the railway station?
Because he needed further training.

Where can a dog go to replace his lost tail?
Any retailer.

How can you tell that your family's Labrador is intelligent?
He brings you your own slippers when you get home.

Why do blind people avoid parachuting as a hobby?
Because it's too frightening for their guide dogs.

★ Related

The Vicar called to see a family who had just moved into a house in his parish. 'Good afternoon and welcome to our parish,' said the Vicar. 'I understand you're related to the Robinsons next door?'

'Yes, that's right,' replied the lady who opened the door. 'Our Beagle is their Beagle's full brother.'

★ How many dogs does it take to change a light bulb?

Clumber Spaniel   The sun's shining, the birds are singing, everything's peaceful and rosy, and you're indoors fretting over some stupid light bulb?

Border Collie   Just me, of course. And have you had the wiring checked recently? OK, I'll do that. And what about the switches? And the wall sockets? No time to lose, must get on, now where's that screwdriver?

Dachshund I would, if I could reach it. As I can't, I'll just go hunting for rabbits instead.

Poodle Yoooo-hooh, Border Collie, mon petit choux, will you do it for poor little moi? I'd luuurrrv to 'elp you but my nails are not dry yet and I 'aven't done my 'air.

Rottweiler A light bulb that doesn't work? Show me where it is! I'll sit on it and crush it!

Shih Tzu Oh come off it, darling. What are servants for?

Labrador Oh, let me, let me! I don't know how to do it but I'll muddle through somehow! Can I, pleeeeze?

Springer Spaniel No problem. And don't worry about a step ladder, I can jump up to do it.

Irish Wolfhound Don't fuss, just give me the new bulb. I can reach it without even standing on my hind legs.

Basset Hound Don't bother. If it's dark I can get into the rubbish bins and no one will see me.

35

Dobermann   Another light bulb gone! I'm going to lose my temper. Grrrrrr ...

West Highland Terrier   I'll get that organised. Where's that German Shepherd? Right, now you do it, or else.

German Shepherd   I would do it, if I could. But that Westie keeps nipping my ankles.

Mexican Hairless   Caramba, eez cold in here, amigo. Get dat light fixed so I can find da switch for da heater.

St Bernard   So what? St Bernards aren't afraid of the dark.

Pomeranian   You've got to be joking. But if I yap loudly enough, someone else will do it to shut me up.

German Short-haired Pointer   I've no idea how to do it, but I'll point it out to you.

Jack Russell Terrier   Ssshhh, can't you see I'm busy watching for the rat in there? Leave me alone and for Heaven's sake do not replace that stupid light bulb.

Greyhound   It's not running away from me, so as far as I'm concerned, it doesn't exist.

Cocker Spaniel Light bulb? What light bulb? Show it to me and I'll bite its head off.

Saluki Oh, never mind that stupid light bulb. Let's go for a ten-mile run.

Yorkshire Terrier I don't care who does it, just get on with it quickly! I need to choose which colour ribbon I'm going to wear in my hair.

★ What colour?

The manager of a men's clothing shop came back from his lunch break to find that his best sales assistant was wearing a large white bandage on one hand. However, before the manager could ask why, the assistant announced that he had some very good news.

'You know that awful purple suit we've had here since last season?' asked the assistant.

'Oh, you mean that hideous thing we couldn't even shift in the spring sale?' replied the manager.

'The very same,' said the assistant.

'You don't mean to say you've actually sold it?' asked the manager.

'Yes I have!' crowed the assistant. 'Couldn't have been luckier, really. I sold it to a blind man who, when I described it to him, said it didn't matter to him what it looked like. All he cared about was how it felt, and he loved the feel of it. It fitted him perfectly, too.'

'Brilliant!' said the manager. 'And he really didn't mind the colour?'

'Absolutely not. He said his wife is blind too, so it didn't matter one bit,' replied the assistant.

'By the way,' asked the manager, 'why is your hand bandaged?'

'Ah,' replied the assistant. 'I think it mattered quite a lot to the man's guide dog. That's why it bit me.'

★ New breeds

Although first crosses are sometimes referred to as mongrels, this is erroneous. In fact these dogs have been developed into new and interesting breeds in their own right. For example:

POINTER/SETTER: *Pointsetter* – a breed often bought from garden centres at Christmas time.

KERRY BLUE TERRIER/SKYE TERRIER: *Blue Sky* – a breed well suited to optimists.

GREAT PYRENEAN MOUNTAIN DOG/DACHSHUND: *Pyradachs* – a somewhat puzzling dog.

PEKINGESE/LHASA APSO: *Peekasso* – an artistic dog with an abstract personality.

COLLIE/LHASA APSO: *Collapso* – useful dog for folding up into very small cars.

NEWFOUNDLAND/BASSET HOUND: *Newfound Asset Hound* – a superb sniffer dog for merchant bankers and business angels.

POODLE/IRISH WATER SPANIEL: *Puddle* – a difficult breed to house train.

TERRIER/ROUGH COLLIE: *Toughie* – a hardy dog that's afraid of nothing.

SHELTIE/PUG: *Shrug* – a laid-back breed with very calm temperament.

SALUKI/DALMATIAN: *Salvation* – a useful dog for mountain rescue purposes.

BORZOI/SHELTIE: *Bolshoi* – a talented Russian breed with elegant, graceful action.

TERRIER/BULLDOG: *Terribull* – a breed prone to minor disasters.

CHOW CHOW/MANCHESTER TERRIER: *Chowmane* – a rare Oriental breed popular with Chinese takeaway owners.

COCKER SPANIEL/ROTTWEILER: *Cockrotts* – often chosen as pets by straying husbands.

BULLDOG AND SHIH TZU: *Bullshitz* – a dog that looks more impressive and sounds more fierce than it really is.

HUSKY/LAKELAND TERRIER: *Hulky* – a breed which, despite the name, does not grow larger and turn green when provoked.

PULI/PIT BULL TERRIER: *Pul Pit* – a worthy breed favoured by members of the clergy.

BRAQUE/COLLIE: *Brollie* – a dog that loves to be outdoors in all weathers.

★ Dog days

The term 'dog days' is assumed to be derived from Sirius, the Dog Star, which rises with the sun in the summer. For that reason it was thought by the Romans, Egyptians and the Greeks to cause the hot, sultry weather. They also thought that dogs were most likely to go mad at this time of the year.

★ Funeral

An elderly farmer lived alone in the Irish countryside with a mongrel dog he loved dearly. At the grand old age of sixteen the dog finally died and the farmer went to see the parish priest. 'Father, my beloved dog has passed away,' said the farmer. 'Would you say a mass for him?'

The priest replied, 'No, I'm sorry, we cannot hold services for animals in our church. But there's one of those new denominations in the town. There's no telling what they believe, but maybe they'll do something for your dog.'

The farmer said 'I'll go to see them straight away. Tell me, do you think £20,000 is a large enough donation to them for the service?'

'Ah,' the priest asked, 'now why didn't you tell me the dog was a Roman Catholic?'

★ House trained

A family bought an Airedale puppy from another family whose bitch had produced the litter. A day or two later, they went back to see the original family to complain. 'I thought you said he was house trained?' said the new owner.

'Yes, he is,' came the reply. 'In fact he simply refuses to go anywhere else.'

★ Morbid

A woman was walking along a street in East London when she saw a very bizarre funeral procession approaching. As it went past, she saw first of all one long black hearse, followed by a second. Then behind that was a woman walking alone, except that she was accompanied by an evil-looking crossbred dog on a lead. The dog looked suspiciously like a Pit Bull Terrier. Then behind this sinister pair, there was a long line of about 150 other women, also walking in silence.

The first woman was so intrigued that she approached the woman who was leading the dog and began to speak. 'Please forgive my intrusion at such a tragic time, and first of all my I offer you my most sincere sympathies with you on your sad loss,' she said. 'I've never seen a funeral cortège quite like this, however. May I ask, who is the deceased?'

'My husband,' said the second woman. 'He is in the first hearse.'

'Oh, goodness, how awful,' said the first woman. 'What happened to him?'

'The dog went for him and killed him.'

'Oh, how terrible!' said the first woman. 'And who is in the other hearse?'

'My mother-in-law. She was trying to rescue my husband, and the dog attacked and killed her too.'

For a few moments there was silence. Between the two women there was an unspoken exchange of heart-rending emotional understanding. The procession walked on, a long, long line of women sharing common thoughts.

The first woman broke the silence. 'Errrr, could I borrow that dog some time?'

'Perhaps,' said the second woman. 'But you'll have to go to the back of the queue.'

★ Why dogs are better than men

Dogs do not think it's 'wet' to express their affection for you in public.

Dogs don't feel threatened by a woman who is intelligent, wears a trouser suit, earns more than they do or drives a fast car.

Dogs feel guilty when they've done something wrong.

Dogs take the word 'no' to mean 'no', not 'perhaps' or 'yes please'.

Dogs miss you when you're away from home.

Dogs don't argue with you over your choice of television programme – they're just happy to lie at your feet.

Dogs, when they reach middle age, will never feel the need to leave you for a younger owner.

Dogs think you're a Cordon Bleu chef no matter what you feed them.

Dogs are usually pleasant to your friends when they drop by for coffee.

Dogs don't boast about who they have slept with and how many times.

Dogs are not afraid to look you in the eye.

Dogs never complain about your driving and don't mind admitting it if they get lost.

Dogs don't mind if your hair isn't done, you're not wearing makeup, or you haven't shaved your legs.

★ Why men are better than dogs

Men can only track mud and dirt into the house with two feet, rather than four.

Men don't shed as much hair.

Men don't feel the need to wee on lamp posts or play with everyone they meet in the park.

Men can open their own tins, and can dry themselves after a bath without spraying water over quite so many surfaces.

Men do not drool or eat cat poo from the litter tray.

Men can take themselves to the doctor and if you go with them, do not normally climb up on your lap in the waiting room and shiver with fear.

★ Men and dogs – common characteristics

Both mark their territory and break wind indiscriminately.

Both seem to smell less attractive as they get older.

Both fail to notice if you've had your hair done or your legs waxed.

Both have an unfailing dislike of vacuum cleaners.

Both take up far too much space in the bed and monopolise the bedclothes.

Both fail to share your fondness for cats.

★ Why dogs are better than women

A dog's parents are very unlikely to come to stay with you, even at Christmas.

Dogs love it when your friends drop by to watch football on TV, especially if they bring beer and pizzas.

Dogs don't criticise you if you come home drunk – in fact they're pleased to see you.

Dogs don't object to you being their master.

Dogs are in agreement with the theory that to get your point across, you need to shout.

Dogs understand that breaking wind in the living room is just a normal part of household life.

Dogs don't notice if you call them by another dog's name.

Dogs don't mind if you sell or even give away their offspring.

Dogs don't care about all the other dogs you've had in the past.

Dogs don't expect you to ring them up if you're going to be home late.

Dogs never make you wait when you're going out – they're always ready before you are.

★ Why women are better than dogs

Women can fetch the post and newspapers from the front door

without leaving teeth marks and slobber on them.

Women will tend to clear your dirty socks away and wash them, not chew them up or bury them.

Women do not have to be walked at 10 pm in the rain after you've had a bad day at work.

Women will usually have just one offspring at a time.

Women's idea of a good dinner is rather more appetising than tinned meat and dry biscuits.

★ Women and dogs – common characteristics

Both look rather silly when wearing hats.

Both attach too much importance to kissing and petting.

Both are very good at making you believe they're listening to every word you say.

Both know nothing whatsoever about football.

Both usually dislike beer, or at least large quantities of it.

Both can eat a kilo of chocolate in one go.

Both are unable to tell you what they're really thinking.

Larger examples of both species tend to have problems with their hips.

★ How to tell that your dog is unusually large

It takes four people to lift him on to the weighing scales at the vet's.

You react to any sound of running water by saying 'Out, now! In the garden!'

People entering your house automatically shield their private parts with their hands.

He can enjoy a drink of water from the kitchen sink without standing on his hind legs

You have stopped putting a water bowl down and just fill up the bathtub instead.

You've had to have the suspension strengthened on your car so it doesn't tip over when he looks out of the side window.

He can not only see what you're preparing for supper but taste it as well.

You suspend your TV from the sitting room ceiling and still can't see it when he stands up.

He can hide an entire soccer ball in his mouth when your children have been searching for it for hours.

You accuse your husband of snoring but notice that the windows still rattle from the noise when your husband has gone away on a business trip.

You take him to the local stables to watch your child ride her pony and the staff there begin tacking him up.

He jumps up to catch a ball thrown for him indoors and breaks the chandelier suspended from the ceiling.

You leave some cream cakes hidden on the top of your fridge and you come home to find them gone, and the dog has cream on the end of his nose.

He can reach out and take the MacDonalds' order from the drive-through window without getting up from the back seat of your car.

Your brand new sofa collapses in a heap after only two weeks.

You take a photograph of your dog with your children and find he fills the whole frame even if you step back at least three metres.

★ Philosophy

DOG: The people I live with love me, feed me, look after me, take me to the vet when I'm not well, supply me with a warm dry house and a comfortable bed, and make a fuss of me whenever they see me. They must be gods.

CAT: The people I live with love me, feed me, look after me, take me to the vet when I'm not well, supply me with a warm dry house and a comfortable bed, and make a fuss of me whenever they see me. I must be a god.

★ Et mon chien

Apparently one of history's keenest dog lovers was King Henry II of France, back in the sixteenth century. It is said that he kept over 2,000 dogs spread out over his numerous palaces, and that whichever palace he was in, he was likely to be followed around by 100 dogs or more. It seems he favoured toy breeds, as that way he could cuddle several at the same time.

★ Ugly

Two men were in a pub discussing their childhood. 'I was so ugly when I was a baby,' said one, 'that my parents had to go and fetch me back from Battersea Dog's Home four times.'

★ Telegram

Back in the days of telegrams in the United States, a Boxer went to a Western Union office, picked up a blank form, went to the counter and wrote, 'Woof. Woof. Woof. Woof. Woof. Woof. Woof. Woof. Woof.'

The dog then gave it to the clerk. The clerk looked at it and said, 'The minimum number of words you pay for is ten, but there are only nine words here. If you want to, you could add another "woof" for the same price.'

'Oh, no,' replied the Boxer. 'If I did, the message wouldn't make any sense.'

★ Legacy

A very wealthy spinster died and left £4 million to her Cairn Terrier. But he was unlucky. Her budgerigar went to court to challenge the will and got half.

★ Lost

A young man rushed into a police station at one o'clock in the morning, very agitated. 'My wife has been missing since six o'clock, and I'm very worried about her. She hasn't come home.'

'Can you give me a description of her?' asked the desk sergeant. 'Height? Build?'

'Oh, about average,' said the young man.

'What was she wearing?' asked the sergeant.

'I can't remember,' said the young man, 'but she had the dog with her.'

'What sort of dog?' asked the sergeant.

'Gordon Setter, that's like an Irish Setter but black with tan points and heavier set, you know, about 30 kilos, has a rolled brown leather collar and leather and chain lead, small scar on the upper left ear, freeze marked on inner right ear, MJ7 4AS, micro chipped with the same code, chip located ...'

'Right you are,' interrupted the sergeant, struggling to write it all down. 'We'll find the dog.'

★ Barking

A couple were visiting some friends they hadn't seen for a long time. As they approached their friends' front door a huge shaggy mongrel began to bark furiously at them, following them step by step. Eventually their friends opened the door.

'Hello! Is your dog all right? We were sure he was going to bite us,' said the man.

'Oh yes,' replied their hostess. 'He's fine. You know that old maxim, don't you? A barking dog never bites?'

'Yes,' said the visiting woman, as the dog snarled around their knees. 'You know that old maxim, and we know it. But does your dog know it?'

★ Black dog

A man was driving along country lanes late one evening in driving rain. He stopped at a pub in a small village, went in and asked the landlord, 'Does someone here have a very large black dog that wears a white collar?'

'No,' said the landlord.

The landlord thought for a while and then replied, 'No, I don't know anyone in this village with a dog like that.'

'Oh gosh,' said the man. 'I must have knocked down the vicar.'

★ Printed pups

A little boy had just been to the neighbour's house to see their Golden Retriever's two-week old litter of puppies. When he got back he ran to find his daddy so he could tell him all about it.

'Tell me,' asked his father, 'were they girl puppies or boy puppies?'

'Four boys and three girls,' replied the little boy. 'And how could you tell? Did your Mum ask Mrs Riley?' asked the father.

'No,' replied the little boy. 'Mum picked them up and looked between their back legs. I think it must be printed on their tummies.'

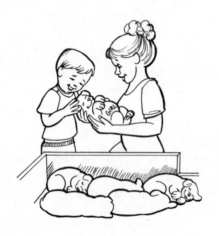

★ Carpenter

An elderly woman walked into a newsagent's shop with her mongrel dog. The dog was not on the lead, and began sniffing around at upright objects in an ominous fashion. The shopkeeper, not wishing to offend the old lady but becoming worried that the dog might cock its leg on one of the displays, decided to draw the old lady's attention to this tactfully.

'Er, what's your dog's name, dear?' he asked kindly.

'Oh, I call him Carpenter,' replied the old lady, 'because he's always doing little odd jobs around the house.'

'I see,' replied the shopkeeper. 'Well, do you think if I give him a nudge with my foot he might make a bolt for the door?'

★ Bar tricks

A man entered a pub with a large German Shepherd. He walked up to the bar and said to the barmaid, 'I'll bet you a free drink that my dog can talk.'

'Really?' said the barmaid sceptically. 'Off you go then, let's see what he can do.'

'Right, please pour out a large brandy,' said the man, then turned to his dog. 'Now, Oscar, what is the structure that covers the upper exterior of a building?'

'Rooooof,' said Oscar.

'And now, Oscar,' the man continued, 'what is the opposite of the word "smooth?"'

'Rufffffff,' said Oscar.

'Finally, Oscar,' the man went on, 'what was the name of the last person to be hanged for murder in the United Kingdom?'

'Ruuuttthhhh,' said Oscar.

The dog's proud owner turned to the barmaid and said, 'There, I told you he could talk.' With that, he downed the large brandy in one gulp. The barmaid called the landlord, who came over to them and asked them to leave immediately.

A few seconds later, as man and dog were walking along the road, the dog turned to his owner and said, 'Sorry, I thought you said last woman. My answer should have been James Hanratty.'

★ Movies

A woman on holiday in a small seaside resort decided to go to the local cinema to watch an old movie. There weren't many people in this small cinema, and she was intrigued to see that a couple of rows ahead of her there was an elderly man with a small Jack Russell terrier on his lap.

The film was a romantic comedy and all through it, the woman could hardly believe the dog's behaviour. During the funny sections of the film it jumped up and down, wagged its little tail furiously and yapped in amusement. During the sad sections it sat on its owner's lap and howled.

After the film had ended, the woman felt she really must go and talk to this elderly man and congratulate him on having such an intelligent and sensitive little dog. 'That was quite the most extraordinary thing I have ever seen,' she said to the old man. 'Your dog really seems to have enjoyed every minute of that film. Absolutely incredible.'

'Well, yes, it is incredible, really,' said the elderly man. 'Especially as he didn't like the book at all.'

★ Drugs

It's interesting to note that in some countries now, vets are prescribing SSRI drugs like Prozac for dogs suffering from mild to moderate depression. This has met with firm approval from animal rights activists who feel that the balance is finally swinging in favour of dogs. This must surely count, at long last, as the first time a drug is being used for animals having been tested on humans first of all.

★ Talent

A famous impresario was visiting his home town and as he wandered about the streets, enjoying the relaxation of being back home again, he suddenly heard the most beautiful singing. As he rounded a corner, he saw that it was a not a human singing, but a small Weimaraner puppy.

'My goodness,' said the impresario to the puppy's owner, 'that's one incredibly talented puppy you have there.'

'Yes, he does sing well, doesn't he?' said the owner.

'Why don't you accompany me to my hotel, so that we may discuss this?' asked the impresario. 'I have the contacts to develop that puppy's talent, and he could make us both very wealthy.'

The owner agreed, and they set off to the impresario's hotel. All the way there, the puppy was singing one beautiful song after another. They settled down in the foyer of the hotel and began to discuss how the puppy's talent could be exploited. Then, just as the puppy had finished singing a superb medley of songs from 'Phantom of the Opera' a large Weimaraner bitch galloped up, snatched the puppy up by the scruff of his neck, and began to carry him away.

'Stop that dog!' cried the impresario. 'she's going to ruin our future!'

'I know,' sighed the puppy's owner. 'That's his dam, I'm afraid, and she thinks he should have a proper job. She wants him to be an accountant.'

★ Guard dog

The owner of a second-hand car business went to visit a well-known trainer of guard dogs, and asked to buy a dog suitable to maintain security at his vehicle compound. Expecting to be shown Rottweilers and Dobermanns, the man was flabbergasted to find that he was presented with a scruffy, shaggy terrier cross.

'Surely a dog like that couldn't guard my property?' said the businessman.

'Ah,' replied the trainer, 'but this little chap is a fully trained killer. Watch this.' He looked at the little dog and said, 'Guard dog, the chair!'

On this command the little dog snarled and growled furiously and with a blinding flash of his teeth, totally demolished the wooden chair in the trainer's office. There were splinters and pieces of wood all over the floor.

'That's incredible,' said the businessman. 'May I see if he will work to my command too?'

'Of course,' replied the trainer.

The businessman looked at the little dog and said, 'Guard dog, the filing cabinet!'

In a split second, the little dog had torn the metal of the filing cabinet into strips and had reduced the paper inside it to tiny shreds.

'Well, I'm convinced,' said the businessman. With that he pulled out his chequebook, wrote out a cheque, handed it to the trainer and loaded the little dog into the back of his car.

Back at his vehicle compound, his wife was waiting to see what he had brought back from the trainer's premises.

'Come and see this, love!' he called. 'Our new guard dog is a trained killer!'

His wife came out of the office and stood over the dog, her arms folded, staring in disbelief. 'You've got to be joking,' she said. 'Guard dog, my foot!'

★ Present

A little girl had just celebrated her Confirmation in Church and to mark the occasion, her parents gave her a beautiful Golden Retriever puppy.

A short time later her mother went out into the kitchen to ensure that the girl was looking after the puppy properly and had placed newspaper on the floor by its bed. She found the girl standing over a puddle on the kitchen floor. She looked up at her mother apologetically and said, 'Sorry, Mum, my pup runneth over.'

★ Shopping

A blind man went into a clothing shop with his guide dog. He picked the dog up in his arms and slowly turned round and round in circles.

'Can I help you?' asked the assistant.

'Not for the moment, thank you,' replied the blind man. 'I'm just looking around.'

★ Washing machine

A woman was most upset when her washing machine broke down, particularly as she had to go out for the day and needed to use it on her return. She rang the plumber and he said he could go round to their house during the day. She agreed that he should let himself in by using the key that she would leave under the second flower pot from the right by the back door, and that he was to leave an invoice on the kitchen table which she would pay by return.

'One thing I would point out to you,' she continued, 'is that we have a very large Dobermann called George. Don't worry about him, though. He's very well trained and he won't do anything to you. He only ever does anything on command. However we also have a grey parrot and I must stress to you, whatever you do, don't say anything to him, no matter what he should say to you. Okay?'

'Right,' said the plumber. 'I've got that.'

Later that day the plumber arrived, found the key, let himself in and worked on the washing machine. Just as his customer had predicted, the Dobermann paid no attention to him, but the parrot – who was flying loose around the house – kept up a continual barrage of insults, swearing and squawking at the poor plumber until he was nearly driven to distraction.

Finally the plumber finished his work and just as he was packing up his tools preparing to leave, the parrot perched on microwave oven and screamed a final foul, four-letter insult at him. Despite his customer's warning, the plumber simply couldn't resist the temptation to say, under his breath, 'One more word, and I'll strangle you, you stupid bird.'

With that, the parrot stared at the plumber with an evil gleam in his eye, and then squawked, 'George? Come here, George! Kill! Kill!'

★ New breed

An interesting new breed of dog is a first-cross mongrel – a Pit Bull Terrier with a St Bernard. This dog will bite your arm off, then offer you a drink of brandy, pick you up by the belt, and haul you off to hospital.

★ Quandary

What's the difference between a killer-trained Dobermann and a British social worker? You'll be able to get your children back from the Dobermann.

★ Guide dog

A married couple decided to get themselves a dog, as the wife was now working from home and the dog would be properly cared for. As the husband was leaving for work one particular day, his wife announced that she was going to take a drive to their local animal rescue centre to find a suitable dog that very day.

The husband looked forward to his return in the evening, expecting to find a charming, shaggy mongrel would be delighted to have been so well re-homed. On his return, however he was somewhat miffed to find that his wife had chosen a pedigree Chihuahua. Not wishing to appear unkind, however, he welcomed the little dog and said he would celebrate its arrival by taking it for a walk to the pub.

Attaching a slender lead to the Chihuahua's collar, he set off down the road and met a friend on the way. As they were entering the pub, they noticed a large sign on the door saying 'No dogs allowed, guide dogs excepted.'

'Oh, no,' said the Chihuahua's new owner. 'We can't take him in there.'

'Yes, we can,' grinned his friend, who was something of a joker. 'Leave this to me.'

The friend took the dog's lead and strolled off with dog in tow, into the pub. The dog's owner followed, wondering what he was about to do. The barman looked over the bar at the Chihuahua and said, 'I'm sorry, you can't keep the dog in here, it's not allowed. Only guide dogs are allowed.'

The friend stared straight ahead, blankly, pretending not to see. 'But this is a guide dog!' he protested loudly.

'Don't be silly, mate,' sniggered the barman. 'Guide dogs are always Labradors or Retrievers. Dogs like yours can't be trained to do that job.'

'Oh my goodness!' shouted the friend, groping around in a downwards direction. 'What have they given me? What have they given me?'

★ On the phone

At way past midnight, an elderly lady was wakened by some noise outside her bedroom window. She went to the window and in the gloom of the street lights she could just make out a dog and a bitch who were mating rather noisily a few yards away.

Indignant, she rushed to the telephone and rang up the vet who looked after her cat, demanding that he do something about it.

'Mrs Jones,' said the vet down the phone, 'it's way past midnight and you have just got me out of bed. Might I suggest you tell those dogs that they're wanted on the telephone?'

'Why?' she responded. 'Will that stop them?'

'Well put it this way, Mrs Jones,' said the vet. 'It certainly had that effect on me.'

★ Newly weds

A young man came home from work one evening to find his bride of three weeks in floods of tears. 'Whatever is the matter, darling?' he asked kindly.

'Oh, it's too awful,' she sobbed. 'I came home from work early so that I could make you my first ever prawn curry for supper. I know how much you love it and I had just got the recipe so I really wanted to make it for you ...'

'Yes, go on,' smiled her husband gently.

'Anyway I had just finished preparing it and the dog jumped up, grabbed the bowl, spilled it on to the floor and ate the lot, and oh ...'

she continued, sobbing.

'Never mind darling,' her husband soothed. 'We'll go to the animal shelter and get another dog tomorrow.'

★ Delusions

For some time, a young woman laboured under the delusion that she was a Kerry Blue Terrier. Although her friends took it as a joke to begin with after a while they urged her to seek medical help. Eventually she sought treatment from a psychiatrist and after several weeks of this was pronounced cured. The next day she bumped into one of her friends who asked her if the psychiatrist's treatment had worked, and if she was better now.

'Oh yes,' replied the young woman. 'I'm absolutely right as rain now. Feel my nose!'

★ Chemist

Halfway through medical school the bright student doctor decided she knew more than enough about medicines to write her own prescription for appropriate drugs when she developed a nasty bronchial infection. She handed the prescription across the counter to the pharmacist and waited. The pharmacist came back a couple of minutes later, passed a heavy paper bag to her and said, 'Well, Miss, that must be an extremely large dog you've got.'

★ Kennels

The owners of a small black mongrel were due to go away on holiday abroad, so sent the dog to a good local kennel. On their return the husband decided to collect the dog immediately, despite being rather tired and jetlagged, so he dropped his wife at their house to begin unpacking and carried straight on to the kennel.

On the way back the dog barked and yapped continually and even carried on once they were inside the house. 'I can't imagine what's wrong,' said the husband, worried. 'I do hope the kennel people haven't mistreated him. What do you think? Is that what he's trying to say to us?'

'I'll tell you what he's trying to say to us,' said his wife as she came into the kitchen and looked at the black mongrel. 'He's trying to say that you've brought home the wrong dog.'

★ Puppy training

Here is some advice given to new owners of puppies by an enlightened Labrador breeder in the UK:

'Take a newspaper – the larger, broadsheet format is preferable – fold it twice, and then roll that tightly. Secure this assembly with two elastic bands and keep it in an easily accessed place. Now, each time you discover that your Labrador puppy has weed on the antique Oriental rug, chewed up one of your brand new, £500 long leather riding boots, dug up your freshly planted pelargoniums or any other such trifling misdemeanour, simply take the newspaper roll and hit

yourself over the head with it, saying 'I must remember to shut the puppy in the kitchen, I must remember to shut the puppy in the kitchen, I must remember to...' etcetera.

★ Showbiz again

A man went into a pub with a Beagle on a lead and said to the landlady, 'This Beagle is extraordinary. He can play the piano.'

The landlady burst out laughing and said, 'Don't be ridiculous – a piano-playing dog?'

'Yes,' replied the man, leading the dog to the piano. 'Watch this.'

With that the Beagle hopped up on to the piano stool and played a wonderful selection of songs from recent West End and Broadway musicals.

The landlady was amazed and delighted, and gave the man free drinks for the whole evening.

The next evening the man was back, this time with two Beagles on leads. 'Hello again,' said the landlady. 'And what can this second dog do?'

'She's a fantastic singer,' replied the man. 'Wait till you've heard this.' With this the first Beagle resumed his place on the piano stool and began to play, while the second Beagle sang a slightly squeaky but otherwise perfect version of 'Rule Britannia.'

'Incredible,' said the landlady, 'you may have free drinks all evening.'

On the third evening the man came in again, this time without the dogs. 'What have you got for us tonight?' asked the landlady. 'A Beagle who can dance, perhaps?'

'Well no, actually,' said the man sheepishly, 'I have a confession to make.'

'Really? And what's that?' asked the landlady.

'You know I said my Beagle bitch could sing?'

'Yes,' said the landlady.

'As it happens, she can't,' said the man. 'I have to admit it. The truth is the Beagle dog is a ventriloquist.'

★ Worm

Some students at a college of veterinary medicine had been out celebrating the approaching end of term for several evenings in a row, and some complaints from local residents had filtered back to the powers-that-be. As a result one of the senior lecturers decided to admonish the students and warn them of the perils of drinking alcohol.

At the beginning of his lecture he placed one worm in a glass of water, and another in a glass of whisky. After he had delivered his stern warnings of the effects of alcoholic beverages on the human body, he then pointed to the two glasses on the lectern. The worm in water was still wriggling about, but the worm in the whisky was lying still at the bottom of the glass, obviously dead.

'Now,' growled the senior lecturer at his students, 'what conclusion do you draw from this demonstration?'

A voice at the back of the room piped up, 'If your dog has worms, make him drink whisky.'

★ Licence

In the days when dogs in the UK had to be licensed, one bright individual decided to get a black and white puppy, as he thought the licence would be cheaper.

★ I say, I say, I say

'I named my dog Corset.'
'Why did you name your dog Corset?'
'Because she's tied up during the day but let out at night.'

'I named my dog Isaiah.'
'Why did you name your dog Isaiah?'
'Because one eye's 'igher than the other.'

'Every time a bell rings, my dog goes into a corner.'
'Why is that?'
'Probably because he is a Boxer.'

'Most days I take my dog out to go for a tramp in the woods.'
'I expect the dog enjoys that.'
'Yes, he does, but the tramp's getting fed up with being bitten.'

★ Top ten things to roll on or in

10. Own basket – familiar but boring.
9. Kitchen mat – can pick up interesting sniffs while doing this.
8. Hall carpet – fun to scratch up into a ball afterwards.
7. Imitation white fur rug in living room – especially when just in from walk in mud and rain.
6. Bird poo – sometimes smelly enough.
5. Cow pat – only if fresh, otherwise uncomfortable and lacking good smell.

4. On owner's bed – only if bedspread has been removed first.

3. On owner's pillow – especially if pillowcase has been freshly laundered.

2. In owner's bed – then have good scratch, especially if moulting.

1. Fox poo – that smell outlasts at least five thorough shampoos.

★ How to take a photograph of a puppy

Take film out of cardboard box and put into camera.

Take cardboard box out of puppy's mouth and throw box into wastepaper basket.

Pull puppy out of waste paper basket, remove cardboard box, three empty crisp packs, MacDonalds carton and several used tissues from puppy's mouth.

Place new upholstered armchair in appropriate position for photography.

Place camera on tripod and switch on large table lamp.

Open puppy's jaws and ensure he has released trailing flounces of armchair upholstery.

Pick table lamp up off floor, unwind cable from around puppy's neck, replace broken light bulb.

Place puppy on seat of armchair and walk back to camera position.

Get down on hands and knees, search for puppy under sofa.

Avoid temptation to cry out in alarm as puppy nips the seat of your jeans.

Remove camera from tripod and hold in one hand, pick up puppy in other hand.

Place puppy on floor, lie down face downwards, lift up head and aim camera.

Remove tissue from your pocket and use to wipe puppy slobber off camera lens.

Get up, remove cat from room, fetch wet paper towel and disinfectant, clean scratch on puppy's nose.

Replace all furniture into original positions and put ornaments back on to coffee table.

Resume original position on floor with camera in your face.

Attempt to attract puppy's attention by clicking your fingers over your head.

Remove puppy from your head, taking care to extract claws carefully from your hair.

Remove your spectacles and make mental note to take to optician's for repair.

Leap to your feet before puppy has had time to assume full squatting position.

Fetch paper towels from kitchen and mop up puddle.

Retire to kitchen, switch on kettle and while waiting for it to boil, telephone professional photographer's studio and make appointment for puppy.

Make and drink cup of tea while resolving to enquire about nearest Dog Obedience Classes.

★ Training

A little boy was discussing his family's new dog with a friend on the school bus one morning. 'My Dad's been training him to be a guard dog and go for any stranger who comes to the house,' he said proudly. 'Dad bought some old clothes at a jumble sale and dresses up in them so he looks different, and then he gets the dog to go for him.'

'Wow,' said his friend. 'How's the dog getting on? Is he learning OK?'

'Yeah,' said the first boy. 'In fact now every time a stranger comes to the door, the dog goes and bites Dad.'

★ Top ten excuses for losing the dog agility class

1. My legs are at least an inch shorter than those of all other competitors.
2. Someone had deliberately created an alternative route inside the tunnel.
3. I was distracted by the flash of someone's camera.

4. The ring stewards had forgotten to lower the jumps after the horses' Working Hunter class.
5. My handler neglected to give me the command to continue while I was on the 'lie and stay' platform.
6. I've never liked Border Collies and they put me off.
7. I was so concerned about going fast that I missed the turn at the end of the arena.
8. The person who had placed the weaving poles was obviously a Chihuahua owner.
9. I was so nervous I had to stop for a wee. Shame what I thought was a pole turned out to be a ring steward's leg
10. Anyway, the whole thing was 'fixed ...' these things always are.

★ True story

An organised-crime gang member in Athens, carrying a home-made bomb in her car, was killed instantly when her dog sat on her handbag, which contained the remote control detonator. Apparently the dog pushed the button with his backside.

★ Welcome, puppies

A client brought a litter of Gordon Setter puppies to a veterinary clinic for inoculations and worming. As the pups squirmed over and under one another in their box, the vet realised it would be difficult to tell the treated ones from the untreated ones.

He turned on the tap, and as he finished each pup, he wet its head.

After the fourth puppy, he realised that the pups' owner, who was normally quite chatty, had become very quiet. As the vet wet the final pup's head, the woman moved forward and said, very softly, 'I didn't realise you were going to baptise them too.'

★ Silly season

A little girl asked her mother if she could take the dog for a walk down the lane. The mother replied, 'No, because she's in season.'

'What does that mean?' asked the child.

'Go and ask your Dad,' said the mother. 'I think he's in the garage.'

The little girl went to the garage and said, 'Dad, may I take Rosie for a walk down the lane? I asked Mum but she said the dog was in season, and to come to you.'

The father said, 'Bring Rosie over here.' He took a cloth, soaked it with petrol, rubbed it on the dog's backside and said, 'Okay, you can go now, but keep Rosie on the lead and just go to the first lamp-post and back.'

The little girl left, and returned a few minutes later with no dog on the lead. Surprised, the father asked, 'Where's Rosie?'

The little girl replied, 'She ran out of petrol about halfway down the lane, so another dog is pushing her home.'

★ Now see here

Returning home from work, a somewhat dim-witted young woman was shocked to find her flat had been ransacked and burgled. She telephoned 999 at once and reported the crime.

The police operator broadcast the call on the channels, and a police dog unit patrolling nearby was the first to respond. As the dog-handler officer approached the building with his German Shepherd on a lead, the young woman ran down to the front door, shuddered at the sight of the policeman and his dog, then sat down on the step. Putting her face in her hands, she moaned, 'I come home to find all my possessions stolen. I ring 999 for help, and what do they do? They send me a blind policeman!'

★ Burglar bungled

A burglar was in the throes of breaking into a stately home. As he was hurriedly stuffing priceless silver into his bag, he heard a voice say, 'Jesus is watching you.'

Startled, he flashed his torch wildly around the room, but could see nothing. Eventually he resumed his work and decided to disconnect all the visible electronics in the room he was in, just in case. After he had finished this, once again he heard the mysterious voice saying, 'Jesus is watching you.'

Again the burglar shone his torch around the room and this time, its beam came upon the cage of a large Macaw, located in a corner.

'Bloody hell,' he hissed, 'who are you?'

'My name's Moses,' replied the bird.

'Moses! Who the hell would call a Macaw Moses?' he asked, relieved and now sarcastic.

'He he he he he,' the Macaw squawked. 'Probably the same people who would call a psychotic Dobermann Jesus.'

★ Devious Dane

A salesman dropped in to see a business client. No one was about in the office except for a large Great Dane who was emptying wastepaper baskets. The salesman stared at the dog, not quite believing his eyes.

The Great Dane looked up and said, 'Don't be alarmed. This is just part of my job.'

'Extraordinary!' shouted the salesman. 'I can't believe it! Does your boss know what a valuable creature he has in you? A dog that can talk!'

'For heaven's sake be quiet,' pleaded the dog. 'Please don't say anything! If my boss discovers that I can talk, he'll make me answer the phone as well!'

★ Cats and dogs present ...

Buy a dog a toy and it will play with it for months until it finally falls apart.

Buy a cat a present and it will play with the wrapping paper for two minutes.

★ Flea dilemma

Two fleas came out of a cinema only to discover that it was raining very hard outside. One flea said to the other flea, 'What shall we do? Should we hop home or wait for the next dog?'

★ Giving pills to cats and dogs

How to give a cat a pill:

1.   Pick cat up and rest it in the crook of your left arm as if you were holding a baby. Place right index finger and thumb on

either side of cat's mouth and apply gentle pressure to its cheeks while holding pill in right hand. As cat opens jaws pop pill into mouth. Allow cat to close mouth and swallow.

2. Retrieve pill from arm of chair and cat from behind sofa. Place cat on left arm and repeat process.

3. Retrieve cat from bedroom, and discard wet pill.

4. Remove fresh pill from container, hold cat in left arm clutching rear paws tightly with left hand. Squeeze jaws open and push pill to back of mouth with right index finger. Hold mouth shut to a count of ten.

5. Retrieve pill from DVD player and cat from top of sideboard. Call partner in from garage.

6. Squat on floor with cat lodged firmly between knees, hold front and rear paws. Ignore rumbling yowls from cat. Get partner to hold cat's head firmly with one hand while forcing plastic ruler into its mouth. Slide pill down ruler and massage cat's throat actively.

7. Retrieve cat from curtain pelmet, fetch another pill from container. Make note to buy new ruler and repair curtains. Carefully brush shattered porcelain and glass ornaments from fireplace and collect together for gluing later.

8. Wrap cat in bath towel and get partner to sit on cat with its head just visible from beneath his left thigh. Place pill in one end of drinking straw, prise cat's mouth open with pen and blow hard down other end of straw.

9. Check medicine container label to ensure pill not poisonous to humans, drink a lager to remove taste from mouth. Apply

sticking plaster to partner's arm and remove bloodstains from carpet with warm water.

10. Retrieve cat from neighbour's greenhouse. Fetch another pill. Open another can of lager. Place cat in cupboard and close door on to neck to leave only head showing. Force mouth open with soup spoon. Catapult pill down throat with elastic band.

11. Fetch screwdriver from utility room and replace cupboard door on hinges. Drink the lager you opened in Step 9. Take bottle of malt whisky from sideboard. Pour large one, drink. Apply cold compress to face and check diary for date of last tetanus booster. Apply malt whisky compress to face to disinfect. Swig back another large one. Throw T-shirt away and fetch clean one from bedroom.

12. Phone the fire brigade to retrieve cat from tree across road. Sympathise with neighbour who crashed into a bollard while swerving to avoid cat. Take last pill from container.

13. Find heavy-duty pruning gloves in greenhouse, tie cat's front legs to rear legs with baler twine and bind tightly to leg of dining table. Press pill into mouth followed by large piece of fillet steak. Hold head vertically (pointing upwards) and pour two litres of water down throat to wash pill down.

14. Consume remainder of malt whisky. Get partner to drive you to A and E, sit patiently while doctor stitches fingers and arm and removes pill fragments from right eye. Call in at furniture emporium on way home to order new dining table.

15. Arrange for RSPCA rehomer to collect cat from hell and ask if they have any guinea pigs.

How to give a dog a pill:

1. Wrap it in a piece of cheese and give to dog.

★ Riddle

Q. What has four legs and an arm?
A. A happy Pit Bull Terrier.

★ Boxing clever

A policeman was walking his usual beat and saw an elderly man pulling a box on a lead along a busy street. 'Poor chap,' the policeman thought to himself. 'I'd better humour him.'

'That's a nice dog you've got there,' said the policeman to the elderly man.

'It's not a dog, it's a box,' replied the elderly man indignantly.

'Oh, I'm sorry,' said the policeman, somewhat ashamed and humbled. 'Well, have a good day, sir.'

The elderly man continued past the policeman, then turned to his box, laughed and said, 'We really fooled him, didn't we, Fido?'

★ Newspaper ads

FREE YORKSHIRE TERRIER. 8 YEARS OLD. HATEFUL LITTLE DOG.

FREE PUPPIES: HALF PEDIGREE COCKER SPANIEL, HALF SNEAKY NEIGHBOUR'S DOG.

FREE PUPPIES ... PART LABRADOR, PART STUPID DOG.

GERMAN SHEPHERD 40KGS. NEUTERED. SPEAKS GERMAN. FREE.

FOUND: DIRTY WHITE DOG. LOOKS LIKE A RAT ... BEEN OUT A WHILE.
THERE HAD BETTER BE A REWARD.

★ Who's here?

An elderly, very well-known breeder of Cocker Spaniels was taken ill
and rushed to hospital. At one point the medical staff thought she
might die, so summoned everyone to the hospital. The breeder's
eyelids flickered as she asked who was there, and all her family and
staff from the kennels called out to say yes, they were. The breeder
suddenly sat bolt upright in bed and shouted, 'You're all here? Then
who the hell is walking the dogs this morning?'

★ Special offer

Notice in a pet shop window: PUPPIES FOR SALE – BUY ONE, GET ONE FLEA.

★ Relationships

Dogs have owners. Cats have staff.

★ Dual roles

In a small town in mid-western USA, the local sheriff also fulfilled the role of the town's vet, having qualified in that discipline before becoming a lawman. Late one night his phone rang, and his wife answered.

A distraught voice enquired, 'I need to speak to your husband – urgently!'

'Do you need him as the sheriff or the vet?' asked his wife.

'Both,' came the response. 'We can't get the dog's mouth open, and there's a burglar in it.'

★ Dinner date

A married couple had not been out together for quite some months. One Saturday evening, as the wife was beginning to prepare supper, her husband stepped up behind her. 'Would you like to go out, old girl?' he asked.

Not even turning around, the wife quickly replied, 'Oh yes, I'd love to!'

They had a lovely evening. It wasn't until they were on their way home that the husband finally confessed that his question had actually been directed at their Dalmatian bitch who had been lying near his wife's feet on the kitchen floor.

★ How to prepare yourself for your first puppy

• Buy a pair of really expensive shoes (Gucci or Jimmy Choo are ideal). Bring them home, remove from box and place on chopping board. Beat several times with meat tenderising hammer, then clip around edges with pinking shears. Laugh and throw them away.
• Take your best white shirt or blouse from the wardrobe. Put it on, go out into garden on a rainy evening and splash liberally with mud. Observe the 'dry clean only' label and smile.
• Put your new duvet cover and bed linen on your bed. Buy a juicy beef shin bone from the local butcher's and bury as deep as you can in the duvet. Scramble around the whole bed and see if you can make all the bedclothes and pillows into a huge pile on top of the bone.
• Take a cheese grater from the kitchen. Apply it powerfully several times, rubbing it up and down, to the flounces on your brand new sofa in the living room. Admire the shreds as they fall to the floor.
• If you haven't done this already, buy a computer and get it hooked up to the internet. Ensure that you have bookmarked a reliable news service as one of your 'favourites'. Resolve to be comfortable with the fact that from now on newspapers are for weeing on or for chewing up.

• Rip up all carpets and wood or parquet flooring from your home and replace with good, old-fashioned, 'easy wash' linoleum. Hire an electrician to remove all electrical wall sockets from skirting board level and replace them at (human) shoulder height. Then remove all objects, including table lamps, from tables and other surfaces and suspend them from the ceilings.

• Remove all food storage elements and, similarly, suspend them from the ceiling, including vegetable racks, canned food stores, fridges and freezers, waste bins and waste disposal units. This is especially important if you are getting a Labrador puppy.

• Talk your husband and children into abandoning socks and slippers as conventional footwear. Persuade them to wear Dutch wooden clogs barefoot instead, although these will require replacement at frequent intervals.

• Put your cat or cats into immediate psycho-analysis (especially Oriental breeds, e.g. Siamese and Burmese). Show them pictures and videos of delightful, gambolling puppies and movies like '101 Dalmatians.' Practise making effective puppy noises like high-pitched woofs and growls. Cover a wooden spoon with fake fur and smack them with it over their noses several times a day. Prepare a sanctuary for them on top of a high cupboard or tall wardrobe, or suspend something strong and inviting from the ceiling (see above, literally).

• Finally, abandon all hopes of a tidy home for a period of twelve to eighty-four months, tending towards the higher figure in the case of such breeds as Labradors, Boxers, Rhodesian Ridgebacks, Dalmatians and especially English and Irish Setters.

★ Police

A police dog van was in a traffic jam on a motorway one warm, sunny summer afternoon. In the car in the next lane there was a family on their way to their holiday in the West Country. The traffic wasn't moving at all and eventually a small boy in the back of the car peered over at the dog van. 'Is that a real dog in the back there?' he called out to the police dog handler in the driving seat.

'Yes, mate,' replied the dog handler. 'Big Alsatian called Dick.' The boy looked again at the dog inside the wire cage at the back of the van, thought hard for a few seconds, then asked, 'Excuse me, but what did he do?'

★ Have dogs taken over your life?

You think it's perfectly OK for your children to talk openly about bitches.

You won't let your children watch post-watershed television but will sit and watch a video on artificial insemination of dogs while they're in the room.

At your son's three-years-old medical checkup you ask the nurse if he should be tested for hip dysplasia.

Your first choice for bridesmaid at your forthcoming wedding is your Cocker Spaniel bitch.

86

You have photographs of your family around the room, but a huge portrait in oils of your dog hangs on the wall above the fireplace.

You've recently bought a harder mattress for your bed so your dog can change positions more easily during the night.

You no longer introduce yourself by your own name, but as (dog's name's) Mum.

When watching TV in the evening you position yourself seated on the floor with your back to the sofa, so the dog can lie on it, rest his head on your shoulder comfortably and still enjoy an unobstructed view.

The first thing you do when you move house, even before you unload your car, is to nail up a sign saying 'Beware of the dog' on your new gate.

★ Decisions

'Why the sad face?' asked one of two women out walking their dogs in the rain.

'My husband says I have to choose between him and my dogs,' replied the second woman.

'Gosh, I'm sorry,' commented the first woman.

'So am I,' replied the second woman. 'I'm really going to miss him.'

★ Eye, eye

Two rather dimwitted types were out walking in the park. One suddenly shouted to the other, 'Oh, do look at that dog with one eye!' The companion immediately covered one eye with a hand and said, 'Where is it?'

★ Last race?

An elderly gentleman finally achieved his lifelong ambition and bought a greyhound. But it didn't seem to have much energy, so the old man got the vet in to look at him. 'This greyhound is very old,' said the vet.

'But will I be able to race him?' asked the old man.

'I expect so,' replied the vet. 'And you'll probably win.'

★ Bragging

A farmer from Texas was visiting the UK and got chatting with a British farmer in a pub down in Devon. They were discussing the respective sizes of their farms, and the Texan was boasting about the size of his property.

'You know, I could go out in the morning with my dog, and we could walk for three days, night and day, and still not get around the whole of our farm,' bragged the Texan.

'Yes,' replied the Devon farmer. 'I had a dog like that once – always stopping to sniff and wee on things.'

★ Tongue twister

A man and his wife were driving in Wales, on their way to collect their long-awaited Welsh Springer Spaniel puppy which was ready to return with them to their home to England.

At one point they entered a small town with a typically Welsh name, consisting of numerous consonants and few vowels. They began to argue over how it should be pronounced, but couldn't agree.

After a few minutes they decided to stop for something to eat and a coffee. As the waitress brought their orders to the table, the man said to her, 'My wife and I can't agree over how to pronounce the name of this place. Could you please tell us how it should be pronounced?'

The waitress put her tray down and said very slowly, 'L.i.t.t.l.e ... C.h.e.f.'

★ Psycho problem

A woman went to see a psychiatrist, very worried about her husband. 'He thinks he's a pedigree Irish Setter,' she said. 'He sleeps in a basket, barks at the postman, and even insists on eating tinned dog food from a bowl on the floor. It's terrible.'

'How long has this been going on?' asked the psychiatrist.

'Several months now,' replied the woman.

The psychiatrist thought carefully. 'You've let this go too far. Your husband will require lengthy counselling and psycho-analysis which is not available on the National Health, so it will be very expensive.'

'Money doesn't matter, I don't care about the expense,' said the woman. 'I'm prepared to pay whatever it costs to stop my husband thinking he's an Irish Setter.'

'But it will be thousands of pounds,' said the psychiatrist. 'Can you really afford all this money?'

'Oh yes,' said the woman. 'He's already won Best of Breed, Best of Group and Supreme Champion at Crufts, and now he's starring in a TV commercial for Pedigree Chum.'

★ Veterinary case notes

1. On the second day the foot was better and on the third day it disappeared completely.
2. Clinic discharge status: alive but without permission to owner.
3. Past veterinary history has been remarkably insignificant with only a 50-kilogram weight gain in the past three days.

4. Between you and me, we ought to be able to get this bitch in pup.
5. He is numb from his pads down.
6. The nostrils were moist and dry.
7. Occasional, constant, infrequent coughing.
8. Pup was alert and unresponsive.
9. Rectal examination revealed a normal size throat.
10. The lab test indicated abnormal lover function.
11. Eyes: Somewhat dull but present.
12. Dog was seen in consultation by Mr Blank, who felt we should sit on the elbow and I agree.

★ Heaven help us

One day in Heaven, St Peter, St Paul and St John were standing around, bored. 'Tell you what,' said St Peter. 'Let's put on a dog show. That will give us something interesting to do.'

'Small problem, though,' said St Paul. 'We've got all the best dogs here in Heaven. There's no competition.'

'Ah, I have an idea,' said St John. 'Let's invite the Devil to compete. He only has badly behaved mongrels down there, so we're bound to win everything.'

The Devil laughed at their idea. 'We would be delighted to compete,' he said, 'and our dogs are bound to win everything.'

'Don't be silly,' said St Peter. 'We have all the finest dogs here. How could you possibly beat us?'

'Simple,' answered the Devil. 'We've got all the judges.'

★ Strange tastes

A German Shepherd walked into a wine bar at lunchtime and ordered a ham salad with brown sauce, brown pickle and mayonnaise. As the dog was eating the barman stared at him hard.

'I expect you find it strange that a German Shepherd should come into your wine bar and order a ham salad with brown sauce, brown pickle and mayonnaise,' said the dog.

'Not at all,' said the barman. 'That's how I always have my ham salad.'

★ Where's Mum?

A little boy was found wandering about at a large dog show, obviously lost, so someone took him to the Secretary's tent to see if his mother could be found.

The Secretary smiled kindly at the little boy and said, 'I'm sure we'll find your Mummy. What's she like?'

The little boy thought for a moment. 'Mostly toy breeds, Poodles and Pomeranians.'

★ Dangerous

Some tourists were driving through the sleepy Devonshire countryside in South West England, and decided to stop in a small shop to buy some postcards. As they entered the shop, they noticed a large sign saying 'Beware – dangerous dog.' Looking around, all they could see was an elderly terrier curled up asleep just by the counter.

'Is that the dog that's meant to be dangerous?' said one of the tourists.

'Yes,' replied the shop owner.' The old terrier woke up briefly, looked at the tourists, wagged his stumpy little tail a few times, then went back to sleep.

'He doesn't look dangerous at all. In fact I'd say he's rather a sweet old chap,' said the second tourist. 'Why have you put that sign up saying "Beware – dangerous dog"?'

'Well,' replied the shop owner, 'before I put that sign up everyone kept tripping over him.'

★ Thinking

An irate exhibitor looked over at the judge in a sporting breeds class after her chocolate Labrador had been placed second to what she considered was a very average yellow Labrador.

'What would you do if I said you're a stupid old trout?' she growled.

'I would disqualify you,' came the reply.

'All right,' continued the exhibitor. 'Suppose I just thought that you were?'

'Well,' replied the judge, 'there's nothing much I could do about that.'

'Good,' shouted the exhibitor as she led her dog out of the ring. 'I think you're a stupid old trout.'

★ That'll be ...

A vet had been invited to an important Chamber of Commerce dinner in the town and was held up during the pre-dinner drinks by a woman who button-holed him at length, asking questions about her dog's anal gland problems. When the vet eventually reached the dinner table he found he was sitting next to a solicitor, to whom he complained about the woman.

'Do you think I should send her a bill?' asked the vet.

'Of course you should,' smiled the solicitor. 'You were delivering veterinary consultation.'

The next day when the vet opened his post at the surgery, he found a letter from the solicitor accompanied by an invoice 'To legal consultation, £50.'

★ Vat's ze problem?

A well-known British judge of Weimaraners was invited to give a lecture to a group of Weimaraner breeders in Germany, to share British views of the breed. When members of the audience were finishing off their pre-session coffee her German host came up to her and said, 'Vould you like to give your lecture now, or shall ve let ze audience enjoy zemselves for a bit longer?'

★ Swap

'Last week I got a beautiful Bull Terrier puppy for my husband.'
'I've seen your husband. That sounds like a reasonable swap.'

★ Who needs cats?

Dogs will cock their heads and try to understand every word you utter. Cats will ignore you and go to sleep.

When you come home from work, your dog will be pleased and lick your hand. Cats will still be cross at you for going out to begin with.

Dogs will give you unconditional love until the day they pass on. Cats will make you pay for every mistake you've made since the day they arrived at your home.

A dog knows when you're unhappy, and he'll try to make you feel better. Cats don't care how you feel, as long as you remember where the tin opener is.

Dogs will fetch your slippers for you. Cats will drop a live mouse in one of them and leave you to sort out the problem.

Dogs will wake you up if your house is on fire. Cats will quietly slide out of the cat flap and leave you to it.

Dogs will come when you call them. And they'll be pleased. Cats will have someone take a message and get you to call back later.

★ Errrrr

Did you hear about the agnostic insomniac dyslexic who lay awake all night wondering if there is a dog?